THE Pioneers

by MARIE and DOUGLAS GORSLINE

Random House New York

Copyright © 1978 by Douglas Gorsline and Marie Gorsline. All rights reserved under International and Pan-American Copyright Conventions. Published in the United States by Random House, Inc., New York, and simultaneously in Canada by Random House of Canada Limited, Toronto. *Library of Congress Cataloging in Publication Data:* Gorsline, Marie. The pioneers. (Picturebacks) *Summary:* Depicts the hardships of the pioneers as they made their way westward from Missouri across the prairie and over the mountains to the Pacific coast. 1. Overland journeys to the Pacific—Juvenile literature. 2. Frontier and pioneer life—West (U.S.)—Juvenile literature. 3. West (U.S.)—History—Juvenile literature. [1. Overland journeys to the Pacific. 2. Frontier and pioneer life—West (U.S.) 3. West (U.S.)—History] I. Gorsline, Douglas W., 1913-   II. Title. F593.G66   978'.02   78-54960   ISBN: 0-394-83904-8 (B.C.); 0-394-83905-6 (trade); 0-394-93905-0 (lib. bdg.)

Manufactured in the United States of America   1 2 3 4 5 6 7 8 9 0

Captain William Clark, Meriwether Lewis, and Sacajawea are being greeted by her brother, a Shoshoni chief (1805)

In the early 1800s, Indian people lived on much of the land that lay west of the Mississippi River. Few white people knew what the land was like. Lewis and Clark, two American explorers, were the first to make the trip from St. Louis, Missouri, to the Pacific Ocean. Theirs was a long, dangerous journey, mostly on foot and horseback. Sacajawea, a young Shoshoni woman, guided their party along the way with her baby strapped on her back. News of Lewis and Clark's successful trip spread quickly.

Kit Carson
Guide on Frémont's Explorations

Captain John C. Frémont
Explorer of the Far West

Jim Bridger
Built Fort Bridger on the Oregon Trail (1843)

Senator Thomas H. Benton
Sponsor of Frémont's Explorations

Soon people back east wanted the land these two men had explored to be a part of the United States. But first it had to be settled. Explorers, fur trappers, traders, map makers, and missionaries made the trip to the Far West. There they found rich farmland, great forests, and plenty of game. Many farmers heard about this wonderful new land. The most adventurous of these became the pioneers. Thousands of them journeyed to the West in covered wagons to settle the new land.

Some pioneers who went to the Far West—Oregon, Sante Fe, and California—were used to moving west little by little, searching for better farmland. Others came from the East or from Europe. If they had enough money to spare, they could load their wagons onto flat-bottomed steamboats and ride in comfort up the Missouri River to the frontier. Beyond the frontier lay a vast unsettled territory.

The pioneers of the Oregon Trail usually began their journey at the frontier town of Independence, Missouri. They started coming in early spring, when the weather was best for traveling. They camped in their wagons outside of the town, where families joined together to form wagon trains. By traveling in groups, they could help and protect each other on their journey across unknown lands.

For most of the year Independence was a quiet town. But during the months of April and May it was filled with excited farmers and their families getting ready to head west. They listened to stories of the men who had made the trip before—traders, trappers, soldiers, mountain men, and missionaries.

The trip by car to Oregon today takes four or five days. There are places to stop on the highway—gas stations, motels, restaurants, and stores. But the pioneers' trip would take five or six *months*! And there were very few places to stop. In Independence they could buy the food, tools, and clothing they would need along the way. They also bought what they needed to start a new life in the West.

Most pioneers on the Oregon Trail drove an ordinary farm wagon. Their supplies were protected from the sun, wind, and rain by a canvas top. It was stretched over hickory branches lashed to the wagon's sides. Though the large wooden wagon wheels were clumsy and made turning difficult, they allowed the wagons to pass over big rocks and go through shallow water without getting wet. Pioneers going to California, and most of the traders on the trail, rode in Conestoga wagons, which were twice as long as a farmer's wagon.

The pioneers' wagons carried food, tools for the trip and tools for farming, clothing, cooking pots, medicine, guns, and whatever household goods and furniture the pioneers could make room for. They made extra space inside by sewing pockets in the canvas to hold small things. But after a wagon was loaded, there was little room left for passengers. And the ride was so bumpy that almost everyone preferred to walk.

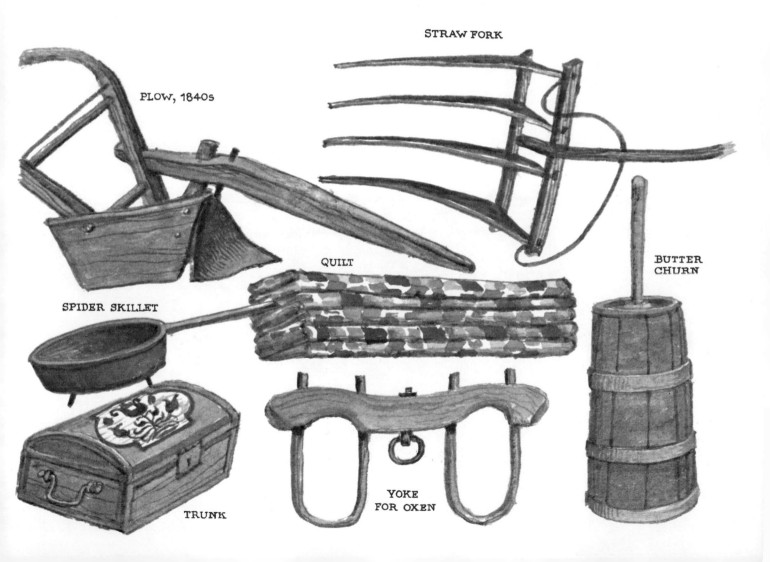

STRAW FORK

PLOW, 1840s

BUTTER CHURN

QUILT

SPIDER SKILLET

TRUNK

YOKE FOR OXEN

Fifty to seventy-five wagons and more than three hundred people—
a wagon train was a mile-long village on wheels, with all the problems
of village life to face. Before starting out, the people elected leaders
to run the train. They also hired guides, who knew the trail well,
to map the best route west. The daily work was divided up.

Some men scouted the land for good campsites, some hunted game for food, and others tended the animals.

Three or four teams of strong, sturdy oxen were needed to pull each of the pioneers' wagons, which were called *prairie schooners*. As they set out across the prairie, the wagons looked like a fleet of schooner ships sailing on the ocean.

The pioneers risked their lives against all kinds of dangers. But they had the faith and courage to try to make their dreams of a better life come true.

They traveled twelve or fifteen miles a day. Women and children walked alongside the wagons, gathering stones, flowers, and berries. Life was different from "back home." There were still many chores to do, and the children had to help. But there was no school! The only classroom was the great outdoors, with its vast, ever-changing landscape to explore.

At noon and at night the wagon train stopped as close as possible to wood and water. The wagons formed a circle to protect the people in case of an attack and to keep the animals from straying. The oxen were unhitched to graze and drink. Hunters brought back game to be cooked. Everyone ate sitting on the ground around the campfires.

As the pioneers neared the treeless plains, wood became more scarce. The children had to gather dry buffalo dung, "buffalo chips," for the cooking fires. Pits were dug for the fires and the pots were hung over them. After dinner, the pioneers amused themselves with talking and games, music—if there was a fiddler along—and knitting and quilting. While the people slept in tents or in their wagons, a night watch guarded the camp until dawn.

Storms were the greatest danger to the pioneers on the open prairies. Wagons were easy targets for lightning. A heavy rain could swell the streams, which flooded the land and turned the earth to mud. Then the wagons might be stuck for hours, or days! High winds could easily blow over a wagon. And a storm could frighten the pioneers' livestock, causing the animals to run off in alarm.

As the weeks passed, the pioneers moved west under a hot summer sun. There was less drinking water and less grazing land for the animals. Hot, dry weather caused the wagon wheels to shrink and crack. The iron rims loosened and fell off. If the train was lucky enough to have a blacksmith along, he made repairs quickly so the wagons could roll once more.

Life on the prairie was very tiring and usually just plain dull. Seeing a stagecoach was a cause for great excitement. During the short time the Pony Express carried the mail to and from California, spotting one of its riders was a high point of the trip.

After crossing many rivers and streams, the pioneers came to the South Platte River. Like other rivers of the plains, it was shallow but dangerous to cross. The river might be flooded by storms. It had hidden deep spots and quicksand traps. The oxen didn't like the water and they often refused to cross. If the oxen stopped moving midstream, a man could drown trying to turn the stubborn beasts around. The rushing water could carry the oxen downstream—and the wagons with them!

As the westward trail climbed higher, it passed through the strange rock formations of the badlands. Soon the wagons came to their first stop, Fort Laramie. In the early years of the wagon trains, the nearby Indians were friendly. They camped around the fort and traded buffalo robes for goods they could get at the well-stocked fort.

Inside the fort the pioneers could buy supplies they had run out of, refresh themselves and their animals, and have their wagons repaired. For the first time in weeks, they could do their laundry! Though they had been over a lot of rough trail—almost seven hundred miles—they had gone only one-third of the way. The hardest parts were yet to come!

In the later years of the wagon trains, the Indians saw the pioneers
taking their lands and killing off the buffalo. Plains Indians depended
on the buffalo for their food and clothing. They became angry and
began to attack more frequently. The pioneers usually tried to protect
themselves by locking their wagons in a circle. But attacks almost
always came as a surprise, and many pioneers and Indians lost their
lives in battle.

After leaving Fort Laramie, the pioneers crossed wild eroded deserts with huge rock formations. Then, suddenly, they reached a broad, green valley—the South Pass. This was the first place north of New Mexico where they could cross the Rocky Mountains. Though they had traveled long and far, they were still more than halfway from their goal.

The pioneers had to be out of the mountains before the heavy snows trapped them there. The oxen were getting tired and worn out. To make the going easier, the pioneers threw some of their belongings out of the wagons. As the trip wore on, many people became sick and died. Some of the pioneers turned back. But most of them kept up their hopes. Young people fell in love and married. Babies were born on the trail.

Pioneers going to Oregon had miles and miles of steep slopes and gullies and huge rocks to travel around. Many wagons broke beyond repair, forcing families to double up. Sometimes they could use spare parts from one wagon to fix another. But the oxen pulling the wagons suffered from strains or falls, and many of them died.

Worst of all the mountain hazards was getting caught in a blizzard. The snow fell heavily in the high mountain passes, stranding wagons and their families. Stuck in snowdrifts, with no place to seek cover, the pioneers could freeze to death or meet up with hungry wild animals looking for food.

When the pioneers reached the Columbia River, they faced more hardships and a difficult choice—to travel by land or water. River travelers had to build a boat or raft and hope it would be sturdy enough to get their wagons and possessions through the dangerous rapids. They had to leave their animals behind.

Those pioneers who wanted to keep their herds to raise in Oregon stayed on the land. They hoped it would be safer. But they had mile-high, snow-capped mountains in their path, and many of them lost nearly everything. Of the 340,000 pioneers who traveled the Oregon Trail, nearly 20,000 lost their lives.

The pioneers who made their way
through the last great mountain range
before the Willamette River Valley
had a wonderful view of the land they
had struggled so hard to reach.

Between them and the coastal mountains lay a beautiful valley with lots of timber, rich soil, and plenty of water. The climate was mild, and the river was good for transportation. Fish and game were plentiful. Most important, there was more than enough good land to farm and to build on. But the pioneers still had a lot of back-breaking work to do.

The pioneers arrived in Oregon in October, during the rainy season. Often working in rain and mud without proper tools, they had to move rocks, fell trees, and chop logs for houses and fences. And they continued to live in their wagons. But they looked forward to the spring, when they could begin to plant their crops. Soon the Oregon Territory was covered with fields and dairy farms and towns. The pioneers had finally made their dream of a better life come true.